Author:
John Malam studied ancient history and
archaeology at the University of Birmingham,
after which he worked as an archaeologist at the
Ironbridge Gorge Museum, Shropshire. He is now
an author, specializing in non-fiction books for
children. He lives in Cheshire with his wife and
their two young children.

Artist:
David Antram was born in Brighton in 1958.
He studied at Eastbourne College of Art and then
worked in advertising for 15 years before
becoming a full-time artist. He has illustrated
many children's non-fiction books.

Series creator:
David Salariya was born in Dundee,
Scotland. He has illustrated a wide range of books
and has created and designed many new series for
publishers both in the UK and overseas. In 1989,
he established The Salariya Book Company. He
lives in Brighton with his wife, the illustrator
Shirley Willis, and their son Jonathan.

Editors: **Stephanie Cole**
Karen Barker Smith

Created, designed and produced by
The Salariya Book Company Ltd
25 Marlborough Place, Brighton BN1 1UB

ISBN-10: 0-531-14971-4 (Lib. Bdg.)   0-531-16996-0 (Pbk.)
ISBN-13: 978-0-531-14971-3 (Lib. Bdg.)   978-0-531-16996-4 (Pbk.)

Published in 2007 in the United States
by Franklin Watts
An imprint of Scholastic Library Publishing
90 Sherman Turnpike, Danbury, CT 06816

A CIP catalog record for this book is available
from the Library of Congress

Printed and bound in Belgium.

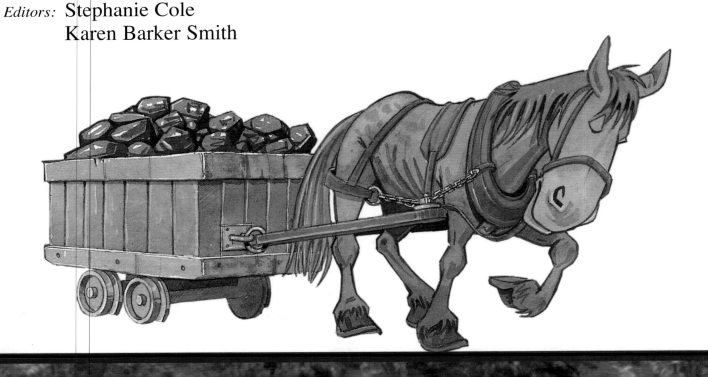

You Wouldn't Want to Be a 19th-Century Coal Miner in England!

Written by
John Malam

Created and designed by
David Salariya

Illustrated by
David Antram

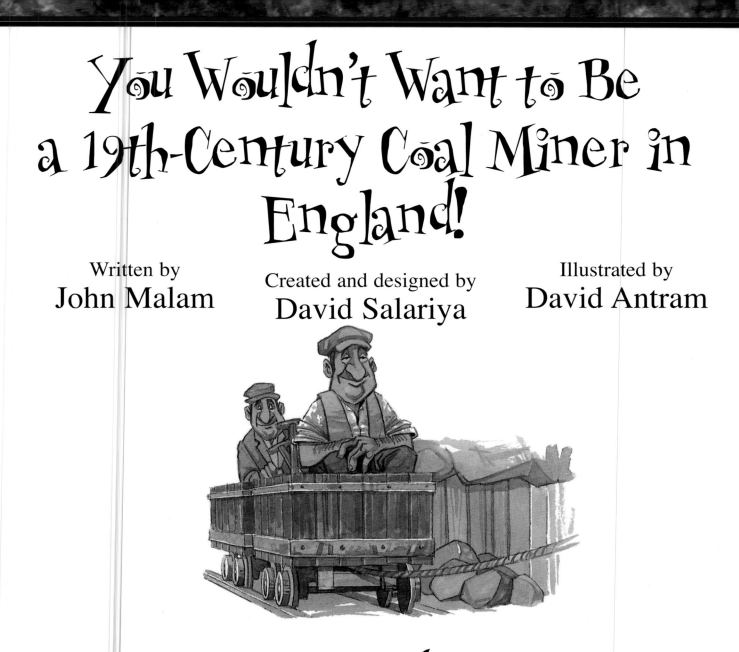

A Dangerous Job You'd Rather Not Have

Franklin Watts

A Division of Scholastic Inc.

NEW YORK • TORONTO • LONDON • AUCKLAND • SYDNEY

MEXICO CITY • NEW DELHI • HONG KONG

DANBURY, CONNECTICUT

Contents

Introduction

t is the year 1869, and Britain is now the world's first industrial nation. In the first half of the 1700s, Britain was an agricultural country, and most people lived and worked in the countryside. Since then, things have changed. Factories were built in towns, and people moved off the land to work in them. Towns such as Manchester, Sheffield, Birmingham, and Glasgow expanded and became cities, where noisy, dirty factories turned out all kinds of goods.

In 1851, the Great Exhibition was held in London. But this magnificent show wasn't just about the goods made by Britain's factories—it was about the machines that produced them, and the power that made the machines work. As visitors entered the exhibition building they passed a piece of coal—a huge, black block weighing 26 tons, dug from a mine at Staveley in Derbyshire. It reminded people that the great advances of the industrial age could not have happened without coal.

Coal is the fuel that powers the machines in factories. It drives steam trains across the land, and steamships across the oceans. It brings light and heat to towns and homes. You are just one of an army of 330,000 miners, or "colliers," working in Britain's coal mines, digging up more than 100 million tons of "black gold" a year. Your life is hard and often dangerous, and you soon learn that you really wouldn't want to be a 19th-century British miner—not for all the coal at the bottom of your local pit!

Child Slavery! The Bad Old Days

Children in the Mines:

TRAPPERS opened and closed trap-doors to let coal wagons pass by on underground trackways.

Y ou don't know how lucky you are! Until 1842, children under the age of 10 worked below ground in Britain's coal mines. It is now, in 1869, illegal to send youngsters down the pit.

BEARERS (usually older girls and women) carried heavy baskets of coal away from the coalface.

Pit shaft

Miners waiting to go down shaft

PUTTERS put lumps of coal into coal wagons by hand.

DRAWERS were children who pushed and pulled the loaded wagons.

Pit props

Some of the miners you work with began work as children or "child slaves." They tell you about the bad old days. There was no school for them. Instead, from the age of six, they went out to work at the pit. For twelve hours a day, six days a week, children worked deep underground in the dark, the cold, and the damp.

Winding engine

We're all slaves here.

The Pit! It's Where You'll Work

You Will Be Given:

No. MEN DOWN PIT

A TALLY. Before you go down the shaft, you'll be given a metal disc called a tally. Mine owners know how many men are below ground by checking how many tallies have been taken from the tally board.

Air holes

Wire gauze

Outer case

Lamp glass

Wick

Oil

SAFETY LAMP. This lamp, or "Davy," could save your life. It will warn you if there's a build-up of explosive fire-damp (methane gas).

The pits of the 1860s are different from the rough-and-ready mines of the olden days. Today's mines are completely modern collieries, designed to extract as much coal from below ground as possible, sort it, and then send it on to wherever it's needed in the country. The pit never closes, and miners work in shifts. Some work in the daytime, others work at night. If you're on the day shift, you'll begin work at 6 o'clock in the morning.

Screening shed

Cleaned and sorted coal

Coal train

THE PIT HEAP is where mine waste is dumped. It's a mixture of slack (small coal) and dirt (pieces of stone and shale).

Pit heap

THE SCREENING SHED is where the coal is emptied when it has come up the shaft in wagons. It is then sorted.

Engine house

THE ENGINE HOUSE contains the winding engine that raises and lowers miners, ponies, and equipment up and down the shaft. It also lifts coal to the surface.

Handy Hint

You'll be lowered down the shaft in an open iron cage. Grab hold of one of its chains, or you might fall out!

Workers' housing

Entrance to mine shaft

Another long day ahead of us...

neigh!

Wharf

CANAL BARGES and steam trains carry cleaned and sorted coal from the mine.

Down the Shaft and Underground!

The Descent:

DARK. You'll be in total darkness for the 30 seconds it takes the cage to reach the pit bottom.

WINDY. The cage falls around 89 feet every second, and you'll feel cold air rushing past you.

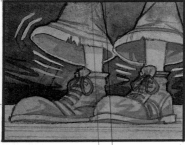

NOISY. There will be lots of noise from the clanking of the cage and the unwinding of the steel cable.

PAINFUL. Your eardrums will feel like they're going to burst, from the sudden change in air pressure.

More coal is needed every year. The trouble is, supplies near the surface are almost dug out, so this means colliers must dig deeper underground than ever before, in order to reach new seams of coal. At 1,640 feet deep, your mine is one of the deepest there is. As you enter the cage at the top of the shaft, try not to think about the long drop below you. Instead, make sure you've got your tally, your safety lamp, and some food. Once the cage starts to fall, there's no going back!

Coal tub

Move Along! Through the Tunnels

Don't waste time at the pit bottom! Leave the cage quickly, before it is loaded for the journey back to the surface. You can forget about daylight and fresh air for the next eight hours. From the pit bottom you have to travel along a tunnel to the coalface. Miners on their way to the coalface say they're "walking out." It can be a long walk—up to 5 miles at some mines, especially those in the coalfield in northeast England, where the tunnels stretch out under the sea. It might take you up to an hour to reach the place where you'll be working.

You Will Need:

FOOD. Carry this in a little container, called a "snap tin."

GOOD BOOTS made from tough leather, with hard-wearing metal studs on the soles.

A DAMP CLOTH to hold against your nose and mouth so that you don't breathe in too much coal dust.

GOOD HEARING so that you hear the sound of oncoming traffic. A pit pony hauling a loaded coal tub won't stop for you!

CANDLES, which are collected at the pit bottom. They're green to show they belong to the mine. Don't try and take one home or you'll lose your job.

MANRIDING. You're not supposed to do it, but you might get a ride in an empty coal tub as a pony hauls it to the coalface.

Lucky me!

Handy Hint

Keep your head down. The tunnel gets lower and lower, so it's easy to bang your head.

Thud!

It can't be much further, surely...

Get to Work! At the Coalface

Your Clothes:

A HAT made of felt. You fix a candle to the brim and work by candlelight.

After what will seem like the longest walk you've ever made, you'll arrive at the coalface. This is where you'll work for the rest of your shift. Hang up your safety lamp, light one of the candles you've brought with you, take up your tools— and get to work! The coal lies in a layer, or seam, sandwiched between layers of worthless rock. It's your job to dig into the seam, knocking out lumps of coal. You'll be lucky if you can stand up without banging your head. Most of the time you'll work on your knees, or lying on your side. It's hot, dirty work.

Your Tools:

LEATHER PADS on your knees and elbows give your joints some protection while you work.

PICK AND SHOVEL. Use the pick to cut coal from the seam, and load it into the tubs with a shovel.

SINGLET, TROUSERS, AND BOOTS. There are no special clothes to wear—just the ones you came to work in.

HAMMER, WEDGES, AND CHISELS. If the seam is very hard, loosen it with these tools.

NOTHING. Some men take their clothes off! They say it keeps them cool. The choice is yours!

That water's freezing!

GETTING CLEAN. When your shift is over, you'll need to wash the coal dust off you. Some pits have washrooms, but most miners get washed in a tin bath at home.

Handy Hint

Count your candles. One burns in an hour, so when eight have gone you know it's home time!

Hmmm

CLUNK!

CLANK!

Take Cover! Blasting Time

You Might Use:

A DRILL CUTTER. It takes two men to use this machine, which uses compressed air to drill holes into the coal seam.

Stretcher column holds up the roof

Drill bit

Air cylinder

It's a long, slow job, chipping away at the coal seam with hand tools. It's been this way for hundreds of years, but now there's a quicker way to get the coal from the coalface—by using coal-cutting machines. These modern inventions will make your job easier—all you've got to do is learn how to use them. They cut into the coal seam, making a line of holes or slots which are then packed with explosives, such as gelignite. When that's done, take cover! The shot-firer will set off the gelignite, blasting coal and rock from the coalface. All you do then is shovel it into the coal tubs.

B00

DISC CUTTER. A large disc spins round on this machine, slicing deep into the coal seam. It's very noisy and makes clouds of choking dust.

EXPLOSIVES. Sticks of gelignite are stored in strong boxes which only the shot-firer is allowed to open. He's the explosives expert.

WATER. After a blast, water is sprinkled over the area to settle the dust from the explosion.

Cutting wheel

Take Care! How to Stay Alive

Luckily for you, coal mining is safer work than it was a few years ago. One of the main improvements came in 1862, when a law was passed which said all pits in Britain had to have a second shaft connected to the first. The owners of your colliery have obeyed the law, and a second shaft has been sunk. Get to know Shaft Number 2—it could save your life. The new shaft is the pit's escape shaft. If an accident happens while you're below ground, and you can't use the main shaft, you'll use this one to return to the surface. It's also the pit's ventilation shaft, taking away foul air. Without it you might be breathing poisonous choke-damp (carbon dioxide).

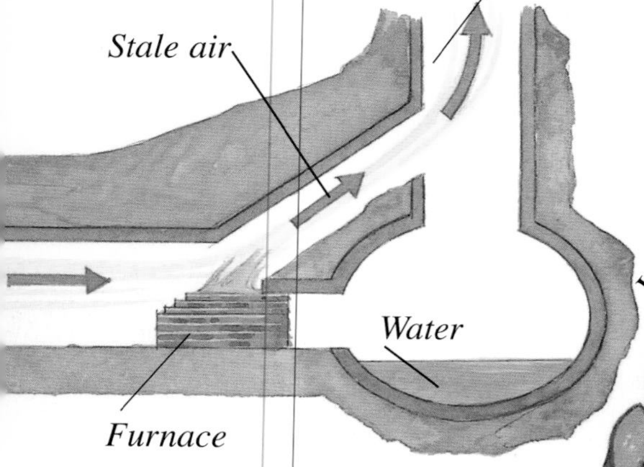

Ventilation or upshaft

Stale air

Water

Furnace

Time to buy a new hat again!

Ha ha ha!

AIR TO BREATHE.
A furnace at the base of the ventilation shaft creates a vacuum. As it burns, it draws fresh air down the main shaft (the downshaft). Clean air circulates through the mine's tunnels and returns up the ventilation shaft (the upshaft) as stale air.

18

Handy Hint

If your safety lamp goes out, re-light it at once. If you see the gauze around it glowing, and the flame getting brighter, that's telling you there's an explosive gas in the air and it's time to leave!

The Rules:

NO SMOKING. If you're caught smoking or with matches underground, you'll be fined. You could lose your job.

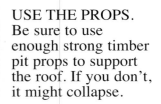

USE THE PROPS. Be sure to use enough strong timber pit props to support the roof. If you don't, it might collapse.

AGE LIMIT. Don't lie about your age in order to get work, or you'll be fined according to the law. Remember, boys under 10 can't go down mines anymore.

19

Help! Accidents Do Happen

The Dangers Are:

FLOODS happen when miners break into old, flooded tunnels. Can you swim?

ROOF-FALLS are caused by explosions and weak pit props. They cause the most deaths and injuries.

EXPLOSIONS, caused by coal dust and the dreaded fire-damp, could blow you and the mine to bits!

DEADLY GAS, such as poisonous choke-damp, is mostly carbon dioxide, an invisible killer.

Even though you're working at a modern pit, where every collier carries his own personal "Davy," and some take canaries with them to sniff out choke-damp, accidents still happen. Some you'll get used to, such as minor cuts and bruises which happen every day, but others are far more dangerous. Pockets of gas can easily build up, and if you come across one you'll either be blasted to smithereens or left gasping for air. It's no wonder that most miners don't live much beyond their 39th birthday—about ten years less than the average age for men in Britain in the 1860s. Mining is bad for your health. Even after you leave the industry there are coal-mining diseases which might be with you for the rest of your life.

You Might Suffer From:

AMPUTATIONS. Falling rocks and accidents with tools and machines might do this to you.

BLACK LUNG. Coal dust in your lungs will leave you short of breath, and your spit will be black.

NYSTAGMUS. Years of working in poor light will make your eyes roll painfully around.

Handy Hint

Take a canary with you. If this little songbird stops singing, it's a sign there's choke-damp in the air.

I'm out of here — see you later!

BEAT-UP KNEE. After years of kneeling and crawling, your knees will be swollen and sore.

CUTS AND BRUISES. Every miner gets these. Don't complain— things could be a lot worse!

BROKEN BONES. These are often caused by terrifying cage drops.

Black Gold! Preparing Coal for Sale

Although most of the time you'll be working below ground, you might find there are occasions when you'll work on the surface, such as when you're recovering from an injury. If that happens to you, you'll probably be put to work in the screening shed. It's a large building where the coal is sorted and made ready for sale. Most of the workers in here are women, but there are also men who are too old or too weak to go down the pit. The women, who in the Lancashire coalfield are known as "pit brow lasses," move loaded coal tubs from the pithead to the screening shed. They tip the coal from the heavy tubs and it falls on to a metal screen—a big sieve that sorts valuable "black gold" from worthless waste. It's hard, dusty work.

Women's Work:

1 UNLOADING. Taking coal tubs from the cage when it comes to the surface and pushing them to the screening shed.

2 TIPPING. Emptying the tubs on to a chute at the screening shed. Each tub holds around 600 pounds of coal and dirt. Some 1,000 tubs a day are tipped.

3 RUNNING IN. Pushing the empty tubs back to the pithead, ready to be sent back down the shaft to the miners below.

Metal screen

4 SCREENING. Agitating the coal as it falls down the screen, pushing slack and dirt through its metal bars.

Handy Hint

Don't wander off! Restless workers are made to stand in a box to keep them in their place.

5 SORTING. Picking over the screened coal by hand as it moves on conveyor belts, removing lumps of stone.

Thwack!

6 CHIPPING. Taking large blocks of coal from the conveyor belt and breaking them into smaller pieces by hand.

7 LOADING. Working at the coal wharf, shoveling the cleaned and sorted coal into canal barges.

Hard Times! Trouble at the Pit

or many years, Britain's miners have demanded better pay and working conditions from the mine owners. In the 1840s, miners in the coalfields of Northumberland and Durham went on strike, refusing to work until their demands were met. Then, in 1858, the National Miners' Union was formed. It's a trade union that looks after the miners who belong to it. You'll find that most miners at your pit belong to the union. You and your fellow miners have decided to go on strike for better pay, and you hope that the union will help you. But be warned—the mine owners are a tough bunch, and they'll try to find ways of keeping the pit working without you. Remember, if you're not working you won't be earning any money, so be prepared for hard times ahead.

Strike Action:

PUBLIC MEETINGS give you the chance to tell people why you are on strike. Try to get them on your side.

NEWSPAPERS will sometimes support the strike. If they won't, print your own leaflets and hand them out.

Handy Hint

Don't forget the pit ponies! Bring them up to the surface, where they can enjoy fresh air, daylight, and tasty grass. It's a sign you're prepared for a long strike.

STRIKE FUND. Ask people in the street to give money to the miners.

BLACKLEGS. Stop miners from other areas working at your pit.

We demand better pay!

WAAAAHHH!

I wish that baby would stop yelling.

The Mining Community

Your pit, like others in Britain, is at the center of the local community. It provides you with work, free coal to burn on your home fire, and, most important of all, a weekly wage. In short, you cannot live without the pit, and neither can the rest of the community. Now that you are on strike, life will be hard. Since you're in the miners' trade union, you'll receive some strike pay, but it won't be as much as you were earning from your job, and it won't last long. And with little money in your pocket, you won't be spending much in the local shops. A strike affects the whole of the mining community. One thing's for certain—you'll have a lot of spare time on your hands.

No, business isn't good these days.

Your Family:

GAMES AND MUSIC. Play charades with your family, sing in the colliery choir, or play an instrument in the miners' brass band.

READING. Catch up on stories you've been meaning to read, such as that new one about a girl called Alice who, like you, also goes under the ground.

CHURCH. Go to church (often called chapel) on Sundays. Methodism is popular in many mining communities.

Handy Hint

There'll be no free coal while you're on strike, so send your children to pick slack off the pit heap.

What shall we do now, then?

Your Recreation:

PRIZE VEGETABLES. You might grow vegetables and enter them in competitions—long leeks and giant onions are favorites.

DOG RACING. You might keep a racing greyhound or a whippet. If you're a gambler you could win—or lose—a lot of money!

PIGEON FANCYING. You might build a pigeon loft in your back yard where you'll keep a flock of racing pigeons.

Strike Over! Back to Work

The strike has lasted six long weeks, and now it's time to return to work. A lot has been happening while you and your fellow workers have been on strike. Miners in other parts of Britain were on strike at their pits, too. For a short time, it looked as though the country was going to run out of coal. The mine owners knew they had to listen to the miners' demands. Officials from your trade union had many meetings with the mine owners, who eventually agreed to give you a pay raise. From now on you'll be earning eight shillings a week, which is a good wage for a manual worker. So, put your boots on, check your safety lamp, hold your head up high, and get back to work. Britain needs its coal miners!

Trade-union banner

MINERS' SONG
You colliers lift your hearts on high,
To God, who rules the earth and sky.
He only can defend your head,
While toiling for your daily bread.

Reasons to Return to Work:

NO HOUSE. The mine owners have threatened to evict you from your house, which they own.

NO MONEY. The strike fund has run out of money, and you have none of your own.

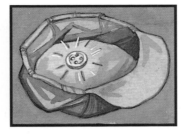

NO FOOD. Your family is going hungry and you need to earn money.

NO WORK. Mining is the only job you know, and you won't get other work.

Handy Hint

Keep smiling! The mine owners might have forced you back to work, but they haven't broken your spirit. Sing a miners' song as you march back to work.

Glossary

Amputation The removal of parts of the body due to injury or disease.

Blackleg Someone who takes a person's job while that person is on strike.

Bob Common slang word for "shilling."

Choke-damp A poisonous gas made mostly of carbon dioxide.

Coalface The part of the mine from which coal is dug.

Coalfield The area over which a deposit of coal is known to exist.

Collier Another name for a coal miner.

Colliery Another name for a coal mine.

"Davy" The popular name for the safety lamp invented by Sir Humphry Davy.

Fire-damp An explosive gas made mostly of methane.

Furnace A very hot fire, enclosed by brick walls.

Gauze Thin wire mesh.

Gelignite A powerful explosive used to blast coal.

Great Exhibition A display of goods made in Britain and abroad, held in London in 1851.

Manual worker A person who works with their hands, such as a miner.

Methodism A Christian movement that began in 1739.

Pit Another name for a coal mine.

Pit heap A massive dump of stone, shale, and slack.

Pit pony A pony used below ground to pull coal tubs.

Pit prop A strong timber support, used to hold up the roof of a mine tunnel.

Pithead The area on the surface right around the mine shaft.

Safety lamp A lamp that detected the presence of harmful gas in the air.

Screening shed The building inside which coal was sieved (screened) and sorted.

Seam A layer of coal.

Shot-firer The man who set off an explosion to loosen coal from the coalface.

Singlet A vest or undershirt.

Slack Small pieces of coal.

Strike When employees refuse to work until their demands for better pay or conditions are met.

Trade union An organization which protects the rights of its members.

Vacuum A space from which the air is removed. This can cause fresh air to rush through and replace it, as in the way ventilation shafts work.

Wharf The place where coal was stored, ready to be taken away to be sold.

Winding engine The engine, usually powered by steam, that wound the cage up and down the mine shaft.

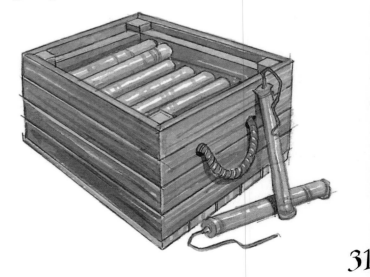

Index

Los Angeles Lakers

Michael E. Goodman

CREATIVE EDUCATION

Published by Creative Education
123 South Broad Street, Mankato, Minnesota 56001
Creative Education is an imprint of The Creative Company

Designed by Rita Marshall

Photos by: Allsport Photography, Associated Press/Wide World Photos,
Focus on Sports, NBA Photos, UPI/Corbis-Bettmann, and SportsChrome.

Photo page 1: Earvin "Magic" Johnson
Photo title page: Nick Van Exel

Library of Congress Cataloging-in-Publication Data

Goodman, Michael E.
Los Angeles Lakers / Michael E. Goodman.
p. cm. — (NBA today)
Summary: Highlights the players, coaches, playing strategies, and memo-
rable games in the history of the Los Angeles Lakers basketball team.
ISBN 0-88682-878-3

1. Los Angeles Lakers (Basketball team)—Juvenile literature.
[1. Los Angeles Lakers (Basketball team)—History. 2. Basketball—History.]
I. Title. II. Series: NBA today (Mankato, Minn.)

GV885.52.L67G66 1997   96-6530
796.323'64'0979494—dc21

First edition

5 4 3 2 1

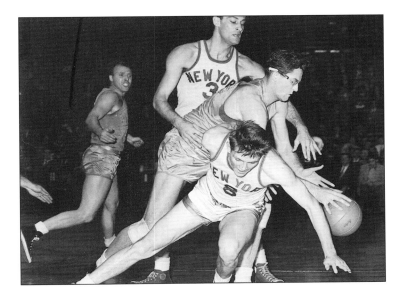

Everything about Los Angeles is big. The California city and its metropolitan surroundings sprawl over an area almost 50 miles across, covering nearly half as much space as the entire state of Vermont. Some of the tallest skyscrapers in the West tower over the Los Angeles skyline, and many of the country's largest companies and banks are headquartered inside those buildings. The city even has a huge full name. Founded in the 1780s as a Spanish mission, Los Angeles originally bore the tongue-twisting name El Pueblo Nuestra Senora la Reina de los Angeles de Porciuncula ("The Town of Our Lady, Queen of the Angels of Porci-

"Mr. Basketball," George Mikan.

uncula"). That name was eventually shortened to the present one, which means simply "the angels."

Big is also the word to describe sports in Los Angeles. L.A. fans pack into two different baseball stadiums in record numbers during the summer to cheer for the local Dodgers and Angels. And in the winter they fill the arenas to cheer on the Clippers and Lakers in basketball and the Kings and Mighty Ducks in hockey.

All sports are big in Los Angeles, but the city franchise that generates the most excitement among its fans, and which has been the most successful in recent years, is the Los Angeles Lakers. A long line of Lakers stars—from Elgin Baylor, Wilt Chamberlain, and Jerry West to Magic Johnson, Kareem Abdul-Jabbar, James Worthy, Byron Scott, Michael Cooper, and A.C. Green—outshone even the movie stars in Los Angeles during the 1960s, 1970s, and 1980s. With the personnel in the 1990s—including Shaquille O'Neal, Nick Van Exel, and Kobe Bryant—the team continues to soar near the top of the National Basketball Association (NBA).

CHAMPIONS OF THREE LEAGUES

The Lakers' story begins several decades ago, before the birth of the NBA. The franchise was formed in the late 1940s as part of the National Basketball League (NBL). At that time, the NBL was just one of several pro leagues struggling to lure American football and baseball fans to basketball. The Lakers played in Minneapolis, Minnesota. They got their nickname because Minnesota is known as the "Land of 10,000 Lakes."

31-year-old John Kundla became the Lakers' first coach—and the youngest head coach in the NBL.

Lakers superstar Kareem Abdul-Jabbar.

With a 28.3 average, George Mikan won the first of three straight NBA scoring titles.

The Lakers won the NBL championship in 1948 and jumped the next season to a rival league, the Basketball Association of America (BAA), where they won a second consecutive league title. Then, before the 1949–50 season, the NBL and BAA merged to form the NBA. The Lakers were the class act of that third league as well. In fact, Minneapolis dominated the NBA from 1949 to 1954, leading its division four of the five years, winning four championships.

There was one big reason for the Lakers' dominance—one very big reason. That reason was a 6-foot-10, 245-pound giant of a player named George Mikan. Mikan was the heart and soul of the Lakers and the first real superstar of pro basketball. The sportswriters of the time were so dazzled by Mikan's talent and power that they referred to him as "Mr. Basketball" and "The Ace." Though Mikan's boyish looks and wire-rimmed spectacles made him appear gentle and studious off the court, he was a terror on the basketball floor.

Today, basketball fans are used to seeing players 6-foot-10 or taller, but in the early 1950s, George Mikan towered over most of his opponents. He also revolutionized the way centers played the game. Before Mikan, most centers spent their time rebounding the ball and giving it to guards and forwards to shoot. But Mikan was not only tall, he was also agile and had a fine scoring touch from anywhere near the basket. He was almost unstoppable. Mikan was so big and strong that the NBA had to change some of its rules to keep him from totally overpowering the other teams. For example, the three-second lane was widened from six feet to 12 feet in the early 1950s just so Mikan couldn't stand by the basket and make layups all night long. But the new rule didn't slow him down much. The nimble giant continued to work his way inside, controlling the boards, tossing in sweeping left-handed hook shots from the top of the key.

"George Mikan is the greatest all-around basketball player who ever lived and the greatest gate attraction," said New York Knicks coach Joe Lapchick. "He's the Ruth, the Dempsey, the Hagen, the Tilden of basketball."

Mikan was not the only reason for the Lakers' success in the early 1950s, however. The team also featured flashy point guard Slater Martin and outstanding forwards Jim Pollard, Vern Mikkelsen, and Clyde Lovellette. All of these men eventually joined Mikan in basketball's Hall of Fame. Together they outshot, outran, outrebounded, and just plain outplayed the rest of the NBA clubs—that is, until George Mikan decided to hang up his sneakers before the start of the 1954–55 season to concentrate on his budding law career. Then the team slowly began to sink in the league standings.

Vern Mikkelsen was one of only three NBA players to average more than 14 points and 10 rebounds per game.

BAYLOR BRINGS THE LAKERS BACK

It has been said that when Mikan packed up to leave the Lakers, he must have tucked the team's spirit into one of his suitcases. Without Mikan in the middle, the Lakers seemed to lose their winning drive. Instead of being great, they became just good. Then they became bad.

During the 1957–58 season, the club hit rock bottom with a 19–53 record. And the Minneapolis fans, who had enthusiastically supported a winner, began to stay away from Lakers games. The Lakers clearly needed a new star. Luckily, they

The remarkable Elgin Baylor . . .

. . . and his Hall of Fame teammate, Jerry West.

Elgin Baylor was the Lakers' top scorer and rebounder for the first of three straight years.

found their man playing college ball at the University of Seattle. His name was Elgin Baylor, and he helped turn the team around.

"Elgin was a cut above the rest," explained sportswriter Jim Moore. "He combined terrific court savvy with tremendous body control and some of the best inside moves ever seen in the league. Now add the fact that Baylor almost never missed from inside 20 feet, even when shooting off balance or from odd angles, and it's clear why he was considered one of the best players of his era."

Finding Baylor and signing him were two different tasks. Lakers owner Bob Short wanted Baylor to give up his final year of eligibility at Seattle to join the Lakers, but the young forward was not certain he was ready to turn pro.

It took several months of negotiations, but Short finally talked Baylor into becoming a Laker. "If he had turned me down, I would have been out of business," said Short. "The club would have gone bankrupt."

Baylor made an immediate difference in Minneapolis. During his first season with the Lakers, 1958–59, the club made it all the way to the championship round of the playoffs, only to be swept in four games by its archrival, the Boston Celtics. Baylor finished the season as the NBA's fourth-leading scorer, made the All-NBA team, and was chosen Rookie of the Year.

A SUCCESSFUL MOVE TO CALIFORNIA

Elgin Baylor could do almost anything on the basketball court, but he couldn't fill the seats in the Minneapolis Auditorium. So, after the 1959–60 season, owner Bob Short decided to move the club to Los Angeles, with its new 14,000-seat arena. Lakers head coach Fred Schaus later recalled that all but one of the players adjusted easily to the new West Coast surroundings. The one who didn't was Jerry West, a clean-cut young rookie from West Virginia.

"Jerry was this small-town guy," said Schaus. "For a while, he seemed in awe of the city and the veteran NBA players who had been his idols in college. Once he got over the jitters, however, he became one of the all-time greats.

"He is the greatest pure shooter the game has ever known. If you sat down to build a perfect 6-foot-3 basketball player, you would come up with Jerry West. He is a man who has everything: fine shooting touch, speed, quickness, all the physical assets, and a tremendous dedication to the game."

West averaged more than 17 points a game his rookie season, second to Baylor's 34.8 average, and ranked third on the team in assists and rebounds. His average quickly increased over the next few seasons, approaching 30 points a game. Thanks primarily to West and Baylor, the Los Angeles Lakers began to dominate the NBA's Western Division the way the Minneapolis Lakers had dominated the NBA when George Mikan was playing. Five times in the years between 1962 and 1968, the West-Baylor Lakers topped the Western Division during the playoffs and squared off in the final

1 9 6 7

Jerry West led Los Angeles in both scoring and assists for the fourth year in a row.

13

1 9 6 8

Coach Butch van Breda Kolff's Lakers averaged 121.1 points per game— a club record.

round against the Eastern champion Boston Celtics, led by Bill Russell and John Havlicek. Each time the Celtics went home with the NBA crown.

Convinced that the team needed a center as dominant as Mikan to capture the league championship, the Lakers stunned the NBA by acquiring superstar Wilt Chamberlain from Philadelphia before the 1968–69 season. Chamberlain, coming off three consecutive MVP years, was considered basketball's greatest offensive player. He had once scored 100 points in a 1962 game against the Knicks. During his first nine years in the NBA, he had averaged better than 35 points per game and had set rebounding records as well. But Chamberlain was frustrated. Despite all of his personal achievements, his teams had only once defeated the Celtics to earn an NBA title. He wanted more championship rings.

When Chamberlain first arrived in L.A., some basketball experts predicted that the Lakers' "Big Three" would never be able to play well together. Each one was too interested in being the star, the experts said. But the experts failed to realize how much Chamberlain wanted to win a championship. The big center changed his game completely, concentrating on rebounding, passing, and defense, and leaving much of the scoring to Baylor and West.

Led by their three stars, the Lakers won another Western Division crown during the 1968–69 regular season and eased their way through the playoffs to the championship round. There, facing them once again, were the Boston Celtics. It was Chamberlain against Russell; West against Havlicek and Sam Jones; Baylor against Don Nelson.

Wilt Chamberlain, the biggest of the "Big Three."

Wilt Chamberlain's 21.1 rebounding average set an all-time Lakers record and topped the NBA.

The struggle between the teams was titanic. L.A. won the first two games at home, one by only two points. Then Boston took the next two contests in Boston Garden, including a one-pointer won on a last-second, off-balance shot by Sam Jones. The clubs split the next two games to force a seventh-game showdown in L.A. In that contest, Chamberlain pulled up lame in the fourth quarter and went to the bench. Boston held on for a 108–106 victory and its 11th title in 13 years. The Lakers and their fans were stunned.

West, who had scored 42 points during the final game, was very upset. "It's as if we aren't supposed to win," he said. "What makes it so hard is that I know we have a better team. In other years, I could rationalize our setbacks, but this time I can't."

West and the Lakers were disappointed again the next season, when Los Angeles lost in the finals—this time to the New York Knicks—in another thrilling seven-game series.

The 1971–72 season finally brought an end to the Lakers' frustration. Despite the retirement of Elgin Baylor, the club went on to set two records, winning 33 straight games during midseason and finishing the year with 69 wins, an NBA record-high that held for 24 years. It was a team effort all the way. Gail Goodrich averaged 25.9 points, West dished out a league-leading 747 assists, and Jim McMillian and Happy Hairston joined with Chamberlain to give Los Angeles one of the most intimidating front lines in the league.

In the playoffs, the Lakers rolled past Chicago and Milwaukee to earn a spot in the finals, once again facing the Knicks. This time L.A. would not be stopped—they dropped the first game, but roared back with four straight wins. After reaching the final round eight times in 11 years, the Lakers had finally brought an NBA crown to Los Angeles.

It would take seven years for the Lakers to bring home another championship, and by that time a whole new cast would be in place in Los Angeles. Those new Lakers would feature the exciting combination of a legend in the middle and a dose of "magic" in the backcourt.

JABBAR AND JOHNSON CREATE MAGIC IN L.A.

1 9 7 5

Gail Goodrich became only the third player to score 12,000 points as a Laker.

Lakers fans thought it would be impossible to replace Wilt Chamberlain in the middle of the team's lineup after the big center retired in 1973. The only man who could do the job, they felt, was a former Los Angeles college star named Kareem Abdul-Jabbar. He had led UCLA to three straight NCAA championships during his college career, and his Bruins teams had lost only two games in those years. Jabbar, however, was starring in Milwaukee for the Bucks.

But before the 1975–76 season, Jabbar became restless and asked the Bucks to trade him. He wanted to go either to New York, his hometown, or to Los Angeles. A trade was finally worked out with the Lakers, and Jabbar headed back to L.A. to play. Jabbar had already been named the NBA's Most Valuable Player three times during his six years with the Bucks. He earned his fourth MVP trophy in his first season with the Lakers, when he led the league in rebounds, blocked shots, and minutes played and was the second leading scorer. At times he singlehandedly dominated entire teams with his patented skyhook, a shot perfected years before on the playgrounds of New York City.

Pat Riley and Phil Jackson, rivals then and now (pages 18–19).

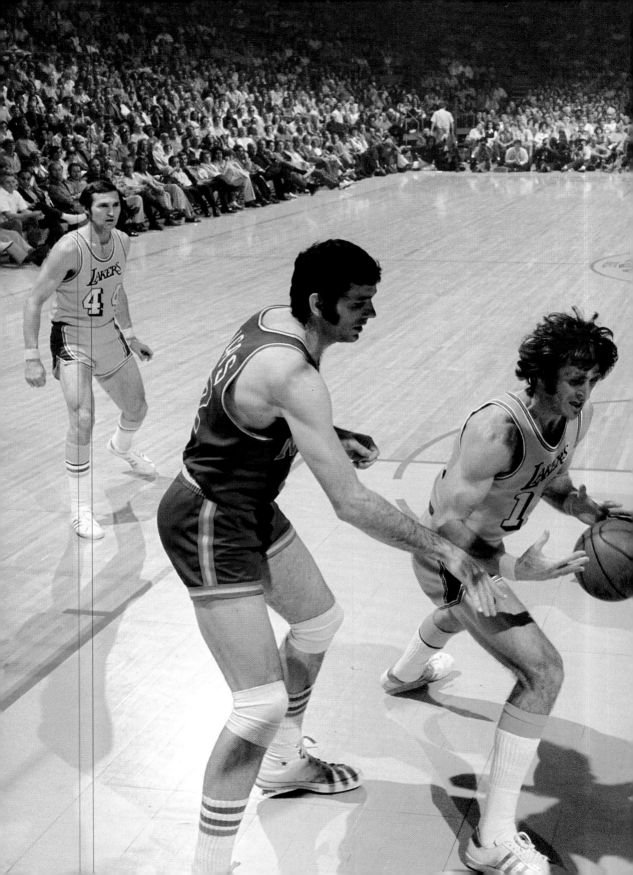

1 9 7 7

Third-year Laker Lucius Allen led the team in assists with 405.

Jabbar's presence dramatically improved the Lakers, but the club still lacked the spark that could make it a championship contender and turn on a crowd in the Forum. That situation changed on college draft day in June 1979. The Lakers had the number one pick in the draft, and team owner Jack Kent Cooke used it to select Earvin Johnson, who had just led Michigan State University to the 1979 NCAA championship. Johnson's nickname was "Magic," and Cooke hoped he would bring some of his winning tricks to Los Angeles and wake up the L.A. crowds.

Johnson was a remarkable player in many ways. He was a flashy point guard in the body of a 6-foot-9 forward or center. He combined great energy and vision on the court with an ability to not only spot an open teammate but also get the ball to him in just the right spot to score. About Johnson's passing ability, one outstanding opponent, Julius Erving, said, "Magic is the only player who can take only three shots and still dominate a game."

Johnson was also an outstanding rebounder and a great clutch shooter. Magic put a new statistic into the NBA record books, the "triple-double." Game after game, he would hit double figures in three different categories—points, rebounds, and assists. Best of all, he made the game look like fun and always wore a smile when he played. "Magic is the only player I would pay money to see," said his archrival and good friend Larry Bird of the Boston Celtics.

From the day Johnson arrived in Los Angeles, huge crowds did pay to watch him put on his special magic show—and they always got their money's worth. With Magic strutting his stuff and Jabbar skyhooking and stuffing, the

Lakers returned to greatness in 1979–80. Along with Johnson and Jabbar, the team featured guard Norm Nixon and forwards Jamaal Wilkes, Spencer Haywood, and Jim Chones. Jack McKinney coached the club to an early season 9–4 record before he was injured in a freak bicycle accident. Then Paul Westhead took over as head coach and lured former Laker player and broadcaster Pat Riley to the position of assistant coach.

Westhead's Lakers sported a hard-running, fast-break attack, and most opponents withered under the pressure. The club, which had been picked to finish no higher than second in its division, raced to a 60–22 record and all the way to the NBA finals, where it faced off against the Philadelphia 76ers, led by Julius Erving.

The two clubs split the first four games of the series. In the fifth game in L.A., Jabbar played brilliantly and spearheaded a 108–103 Laker win. But the big center severely sprained an ankle and was unavailable for the sixth game in Philadelphia. Who was going to replace Jabbar in the middle? Coach Westhead decided to try a trick of his own and asked Magic Johnson to shift positions. Magic hadn't played center since high school, but he was willing to do his best. His best turned out to be 42 points, 15 rebounds, seven assists, three steals, and one blocked shot. Behind Magic and Jamaal Wilkes, the Lakers turned a 60–60 halftime tie into a 123–107 romp. Los Angeles was once again atop the NBA.

1 9 7 9

Norm Nixon grabbed 82 steals to lead the Lakers for the second season in a row.

The magical Earvin Johnson.

PAT RILEY LEADS "THE TEAM OF THE '80S"

With their victory in the 1980 playoffs, the Lakers began a decade of league dominance that would rival the success enjoyed by only two earlier teams in NBA history—the Minneapolis Lakers in the 1950s and the Boston Celtics in the 1960s. Sportswriters began to call the Lakers "The Team of the '80s."

They deserved the title. Los Angeles made eight appearances in the championship series during the decade and came away with five NBA crowns, including back-to-back championships in 1987 and 1988. It was the first time in 19 years that any NBA club had won consecutive titles.

One change in the Laker organization was instrumental in the team's incredible success. After a dismal start to the 1981–82 season, Coach Westhead was asked to step aside, and his assistant Pat Riley took over. The Lakers exploded under Riley, winning 11 of the next 13 games, and they never looked back. They finished the season with a 57–25 record, then breezed through the playoffs winning 12 of 14 contests, including a then NBA-record nine wins in a row. Just like that, Riley had garnered a world title in his first year as head coach.

During his nine years at the Lakers' helm, Riley guided the club to the NBA finals eight times and to four league championships. He reached the 500-victory mark faster than any other coach in NBA history and ranks second as the coach with the highest lifetime winning percentage.

Despite his outstanding record, Riley was only once named NBA Coach of the Year while in L.A. Sportswriters

1 9 8 2

Mitch Kupchak was 11-11 for a perfect shooting performance in a game against San Antonio.

said, "Riley doesn't have to do much. Anybody could win with all the talent his teams have had." It was foolish criticism. Pat Riley didn't just inherit great talent on his teams; he picked players that fit the style of basketball he wanted his teams to play and then molded those players into cohesive, winning units.

"All I care about is creating an environment in which the talent can flourish," he commented. "That means all 12 of our individuals. I have to know as much as possible about each one, to motivate them, to be able to draw them together, to know how to serve them best. I have a role—to organize, to direct, to put the players in position to win. But, then, they're going to do the winning, not me."

When Riley took command of the Lakers, the club was built around Kareem Abdul-Jabbar and Magic Johnson. These two players remained the cornerstones of the team during the 1980s, but their supporting cast changed considerably. Under Riley's direction, such players as James Worthy, Byron Scott, Michael Cooper, A.C. Green, and Mychal Thompson arrived in L.A. via trades or the draft, and each was melded into the Laker system. It is a testament to Riley's coaching genius that he was able to maintain the championship caliber of his club while it underwent such drastic personnel shifts.

DUNLEAVY TAKES COMMAND

Following the 1989–90 season, Pat Riley decided to step down as Lakers coach to become a basketball analyst on television. The Lakers' reins were handed to former NBA player Mike Dunleavy. He had been a scrapper during his playing days, and Dunleavy promised that his new team would have the same personality.

Basketball experts figured that the Lakers would suffer an immediate decline during the 1990–91 season. But they were wrong. "The Lakers aren't going away," Magic Johnson said with assurance. "Anyone who thinks we can't keep winning championships doesn't know what we're about."

Indeed, during Dunleavy's first year at the helm, the Lakers came close to winning another NBA title. They finished the year with the second-best record in the Pacific Division, behind the Portland Trail Blazers, then whipped the Blazers in the playoffs to reach the championship round against Michael Jordan and the Chicago Bulls. The younger, faster Bulls outran Los Angeles in the finals, however, and ended the Lakers' hopes for another title.

Despite the loss, there was clearly reason for optimism in Los Angeles. Dunleavy had developed a new passing attack for his team and had added three new stars to the L.A. cast. One was veteran forward Sam Perkins, who arrived as a free agent before the 1990–91 season. The other two were center Vlade Divac, an outstanding player from Yugoslavia, and power forward Elden Campbell, a rookie from Clemson. The new talent, combined with longtime winners Magic Johnson, Byron Scott, and James Worthy, promised to make the Lakers "The Team of the '90s" as well.

But the optimism felt by L.A. players and fans diminished on November 7, 1991, and was replaced by shock and sadness. That was the day that Magic Johnson made a stunning announcement. He told a hushed crowd of reporters that he

1 9 9 0

A.C. Green reigned as team rebounding leader for the fourth straight year.

Singular sensation Shaquille O'Neal (pages 26–27).

had been tested positive for HIV, the virus that causes the disease AIDS. He chose to retire from the NBA.

Taking over at point guard, Sedale Threatt led the Lakers in points, assists, steals, and minutes played.

SHAQ COMES TO HOLLYWOOD

Though retired, Magic Johnson was selected to play in the 1992 All-Star game. He played so well that he was voted the game's MVP. Magic played in the Barcelona Olympics in the summer of 1992, helping the U.S. win a gold medal. Johnson then announced that he was returning to play full time for the Lakers. But exhausted after the 1992–93 preseason, he again retired.

After Magic's second departure, the Lakers began rebuilding. Dunleavy stepped down and was replaced at head coach by Laker assistant Dennis Pfund. Green and Scott were let go, Perkins was traded, and Worthy retired. Vlade Divac emerged as the Lakers' top scorer, but the new-look Lakers' 33–49 record in 1993–94 was their worst in nearly two decades, despite the fact that Magic returned late during the season to take over for Pfund as head coach.

Lakers owner Jerry Buss finally committed to a long-term rebuilding plan when he named Del Harris as the club's head coach and began a youth movement that would take several years to complete. That movement saw several talented players come and go, including Sedale Threatt, Cedric Ceballos, Anthony Peeler, and Doug Christie. At one time or another, each of these players was considered a key part of the Lakers' future. But as the rebuilding progressed, the players who stayed on as the foundation of the Lakers' future were Elden Campbell, 1993 draft pick Nick Van Exel, and 1994 first-round draft pick Eddie Jones.

The 6-foot-11 Campbell continued to improve every year. He became a skilled shot blocker and rebounder and was one of only 21 players in NBA history to increase his scoring average in each of his first six seasons in the league. Van Exel, a point guard, provided backcourt balance and proved to be an excellent floor general, dishing out assists and dropping three-point shots. Jones became a ball-stealing expert who could play either guard or forward, complementing the strengths of Campbell and Van Exel. The Lakers had three of the five pieces of their puzzle, and in the 1995–96 off-season, they acquired the final two pieces. First they signed one of the most dominant players in the NBA, Shaquille O'Neal, who was destined to join the ranks of Chamberlain and Jabbar as another great Laker center. Then they traded Divac to Charlotte for the Hornets' 1996 first-round draft selection, high school phenom Kobe Bryant.

Bryant had been a high school star in Ardmore, Pennsylvania, and at 18 years and two months old, he became the second-youngest player ever in the NBA. Bryant was the all-time leading scorer in southeastern Pennsylvania history, passing Hall of Famer and former Laker Wilt Chamberlain.

"I think he's going to be a wonderful player, a great player," said mentor and teammate Eddie Jones. "One-on-one, he's a handful to try to control."

"There is nothing about him that has not impressed me," said coach Harris of Bryant, who played more in his rookie year than anyone expected, a result of his quick adjustment

1 9 9 6

Elden Campbell became the first Laker in 14 years to record more than 200 blocked shots in a season.

29

The phenomenal Kobe Bryant.

Powerful Nick Van Exel.

1 9 9 7

Travis Knight joined Kobe Bryant on the NBA All-Rookie second team.

to the NBA game. "He is an incredible talent who will be a prominent part of this team someday."

Bryant was big news, but even bigger news was the signing of Orlando Magic free agent Shaquille O'Neal. In his fourth season, the 7-foot-1, 300-pound O'Neal had ranked among the top 10 in the NBA in scoring, blocked shots, and field-goal percentage every year. He was one of the most dominant players in years, having won many of the league's top honors, including Rookie of the Year. But Shaq had never won an NBA championship, which was what he hoped to bring to L.A.

"He wants to improve, and he wants to win games," said Harris of his new star. "He's got such a lighthearted spirit about him that he can break up a pressure situation. That kind of personality is going to wear very well with our team."

The 1996-97 season was a bit of a letdown when Shaq injured his knee and missed a third of the season. But he returned to dominate the first round of the playoffs, with the Lakers beating the favored Portland Trail Blazers. In the second round, however, league MVP Karl Malone and a veteran-laden Utah Jazz club proved to be too much for the young Lakers, who lost the semifinal series in five games. Still, the Lakers' starting lineup averages younger than 26 years old. If they continue to make the most of that energy, and if they can weather the free-agency tide, the Lakers are sure to dominate the NBA for years to come.